A MARRIAGE
PREPARATION
PROGRAM **FOR**
CATHOLIC
COUPLES

Strong Foundations

COUPLE'S BOOK

HOLLY B. CARBO

MANDI M. CHAPMAN

TWENTY-THIRD PUBLICATIONS
twentythirdpublications.com

TWENTY-THIRD PUBLICATIONS
One Montauk Avenue, Suite 200
New London, CT 06320
(860) 437-3012 or (800) 321-0411
www.twentythirdpublications.com

Second Printing 2017

IMPRIMATUR
+ Most Reverend Ronald P. Herzog
Bishop of Alexandria
February 2, 2012

ISBN 978-1-58595-879-5
Library of Congress Control Number: 2012939498

IMAGE CREDITS
PAGE 1: iStockphoto/wragg • **PAGE 3**: Photos.com/iofoto • **PAGE 4**: iStockphoto/aldomurillo • **PAGE 6**: Photos.com/Ingvar Bjork • **PAGE 7**: Photos.com/gollykim • **PAGE 9**: Photos.com/SimonKr d.o.o. • **PAGE 15**: iStockphoto/mediaphotos • **PAGE 16**: Photos.com/Comstock Images • **PAGE 19**: Photos.com/Comstock • **PAGE 22**: Photos.com/Comstock Images • **PAGE 24**: Photos.com/Stockbyte • **PAGE 26**: Photos.com/Stockbyte • **PAGE 27**: iStockphoto/catscandotcom • **PAGE 28**: *(top)* Photos.com/Elzbieta Sekowska; *(bottom)* Photos.com/Thinkstock • **PAGE 31**: Photos.com/Jupiterimages • **PAGE 33**: Photos.com/Andreas Rodriguez • **PAGE 34**: Photos.com/Tana Minnick • **PAGE 37**: Photos.com/RusN • **PAGE 38**: Photos.com/Thinkstock Images • **PAGE 39**: Corbis/SuperStock • **PAGE 42**: Fancy Collection/SuperStock • **PAGE 44**: Photos.com/George Doyle • **PAGE 45**: *(top)* iStockphoto/pixhook; *(bottom)* Photos.com/Tatiana Morozova • **PAGE 48**: iStockphoto/vernonwiley • **PAGE 54**: Photos.com/Jupiterimages

Printed in the U.S.A.

A division of Bayard, Inc.

Contents

Introduction

Marriage preparation is not wedding preparation. Marriage preparation is learning how to live life as a couple after the cake is cut and the honeymoon is over. That's when real marriage begins.

Strong Foundations is a workshop designed to prepare you for the hard work of creating a loving marriage with God at its center. While this seminar cannot ensure a lifetime of marital perfection, it will realistically address the issues important in a lasting marriage. You will learn about yourself and your partner in a way few couples experience prior to marriage. In addition, you will learn the basic skills needed to handle the normal (and not-so-normal) transitions involved in marriage.

In these pages, you will find many of the issues the United States Conference of Catholic Bishops suggests engaged couples consider prior to marriage.

Some of you may think a marriage preparation program is unnecessary. However, no one goes to the altar, looks at their bride or groom, and says, "You are a wonderful first wife (husband). I will love you until we file for divorce." Yet that's the reality for half of all marriages.

Strong Foundations will help you to discern whether you should walk away now, or proceed to the altar. Through this process, you will find questions you need to ask before going to the altar, skills necessary to make a marriage more fulfilling, and self-knowledge to approach marriage realistically. It will help you to understand what it really means to get married in the Church before God and family. And, if you are open, it will provide a strong foundation on which to build your marriage and family. ∎

PRAYER

Dear Lord,

*I come before You today
as a sign of my commitment
to You and my future spouse.
I ask that You keep my
heart and mind open
to what You will share
with me today through the
topics in this workshop.
I pray that I am able
to discern the wisdom from
this workshop that I need to
make my marriage an enduring
one with You at its center.
Amen.*

So that the "I do" of the spouses may be a free and responsible act and so that the marriage covenant may have solid and lasting human and Christian foundations, **preparation for marriage is of prime importance**. [CATECHISM 1632]

Choice

BEFORE YOU BEGIN ✳ READINESS

REASONS TO RECONSIDER MARRIAGE

Marriage is a choice. Until the minute
you are face to face before the priest committing yourselves to God
and each other, you have the opportunity to say "I don't." Hopefully,
though, you will have decided "I do" or "I don't" before that life-
changing moment.

Marriage readiness is all about a couple's perception of what they
bring to the marriage table and how well they think they can handle
married life. Be forewarned: no one plans on divorce, but it happens
anyway. It is important that you take a hard look at what makes
marriage challenging, difficult, or troublesome before choosing to get
married and stay married.

In marriage, "two…become one flesh" (Matthew 19:5). Know-

4

ing how your values and beliefs coincide or collide is important to understanding just how calm or calamitous that joining will be. Yet growing from a focus on self to a focus on another is an integral part of choosing to marry.[20]

When you become one with your partner, it doesn't mean that everything suddenly becomes easy and all differences melt away. It means you have to work with what you have, find a way to make two people into one family, and compromise when you need to. It's backbreaking work.

When faced with the knowledge that you will become one with your intended spouse, can you live with him or her just as he or she is now? Can you live the rest of your life accepting your differences and, in fact, embracing them? Without changing him or her? Can you accept in-laws, his habits, her compulsions, his way of doing things, her mother's way of doing things? Are you able to see the influence of the way you were raised and integrate the best parts into your marriage while rejecting the unwanted parts? Are you open to finding ways of replacing bad relationship habits with healthy ones?

Statistics on marriage are staggering. Couples hear about the success rate (and failure rate) of marriage in magazines, newspapers, on TV, and on the web. However, most people optimistically believe those statistics relate to someone else, to some other couple. Few couples recognize that they could quite easily fall into the marriage failure category. And because couples don't recognize this, they do nothing to prevent failure.

You have to realistically recognize just how easy it is for a marriage to fail. Then you must make a conscious choice to work against failure if you want a successful marriage. Choosing to marry is actively working against the statistics, not passively assuming you won't be one.

Or it's choosing to walk away now, before the vows. Sometimes the most adult, responsible decision a couple can make is to say "I don't." If you aren't ready or if the foundation of your relationship is shaky, don't make a lifelong commitment because the florist has been paid. Skip the hurt, anger, anxiety, and scars of divorce, and postpone or cancel the wedding. If you *aren't* ready, choose wisely.

If you *are* ready, choose wisely. ■

Before you begin

Before you begin this marriage preparation workshop, it is important for you to focus on why you are here and why you have chosen the person at your side to be your future spouse. Bring to mind what has brought you to this point in your life: You are planning a wedding, a lifetime of marriage, and a family with the person next to you.

What meaning does this have for you?

This first exercise is all about you two and your intent to be married. Your response to this exercise should not only remain in the forefront of your mind during this seminar, but also throughout your married life.

>> **What makes you want to marry the person sitting next to you?**

Affirm our commitment to a strong and lasting relationship
New perspectives
Collaborative strengths

>> **What about this person makes him or her the right mate for you?**

Good communication, similar goals, willing to compromise, romantic spark
Laugh more than cry
Inspiration, support & appreciation

>> **Why are you seeking marriage in the Catholic Church?**

Sacrament of marriage

Readiness

No one approaches marriage planning to divorce. Everyone wants and expects to live "happily ever after." But divorce happens. No one can discuss what makes a marriage successful without talking about what makes it unsuccessful. The more you know about why divorce happens, the more prepared you are to avoid the problems that lead to divorce.

Here are some things you need to know about divorce.

- Almost half of marriages end in divorce. But did you know the numbers change with age?
  - » 50% of marriages for people aged 18 and under end in divorce.[1]
  - » Divorce for people 18 and under occurs within 10 years.[2]
  - » 40% of marriages for people 20 and under end in divorce.[1]
  - » Only 24% of marriages for people 25 and older end in divorce.[1]
- Two-thirds of divorced people say they wish their spouse had worked harder to save the marriage.[3]
- Couples who live together before marriage are more likely to divorce than those who do not.[3, 5, 6, 7, 10, 16]
- Shared religious activities are more important to the success of a marriage than shared religions.[3]
- Divorce rates are higher in urban areas than in rural areas.[4]
- Those raised in single parent homes are much more likely to divorce.[8]
- Children of divorce are themselves more likely to divorce.[9, 10, 16]
- Divorce rates are rising.[10]
- The divorce rate of remarriages is higher than first marriages.[10, 11]

> The intimate union of marriage, as a mutual giving of two persons, and the good of the children demand **total fidelity** from the spouses and require **an unbreakable unity** between them.
>
> [GAUDIUM ET SPES, #48]

Every step you take now to prepare properly for marriage gives you a greater chance of marital success. The more you know about your spouse, and the more you know about how to communicate with your spouse, the less chance you have of being a statistic!

7

Reasons to reconsider marriage

Each of you can probably list many reasons why you should spend a lifetime with the person next to you. Yet some couples could avoid divorce simply by avoiding a doomed marriage. You are here because you have been given the opportunity to discern the vocation of marriage before you say "I do." Before agreeing to spend a lifetime together, carefully consider if there are any issues that may prove insurmountable in your marriage. Reflect on the following lists and remember, sometimes there's a good reason for getting cold feet!

You may want to reconsider marriage if any of the following refer to you.

- You have few or no common values.
- You think you can change him/her once you're married.
- All you do is fight.
- One or both of you struggle with persistent drug or alcohol abuse.
- Physical, mental, emotional, and/or psychological abuse occur in your relationship.

The following should be considered a poor motivation for marriage.

- It is on your checklist of things to do before age 30 (or after college, etc.).
- You have a baby, and it seems like the right thing to do.
- You want to get out of the house.
- All of your friends are doing it.
- Marriage seems convenient.
- You think it's a financially good choice (two incomes are better than one; you want someone to support you; etc.).
- You are happy living together.
- Your parents want you to stop living together.
- You want to have your marriage blessed because you are having problems.

Conversation starters

Did you have a previous reluctance or hesitation to marry your fiancé(e)? If so, why?

If you have had a previous hesitation to marry, have your issues been resolved? If they haven't, how do you plan to resolve them?

What, if anything, have you withheld from your future spouse that would prevent him or her from marrying you?

On a scale from 1 to 10, with 1 being "NOT AT ALL READY" and 10 being "VERY READY," how would you rate your readiness for marriage? _____ Why?

Trust in the Lord with all your heart and lean not on your own understanding; in all your ways acknowledge Him, and He will make your paths straight.

[PROVERBS 3:5–6]

Core

VALUES ✳ THE VALUES WORKSHEET

MY VALUES ✳ MY VALUES IN RELATIONSHIP

Values

Marriage is serious business. It's why you're here, why you waited to marry just the right person, and why you are planning to be married in the Church. It's a serious undertaking that takes love and commitment. But it takes so much more than just sweet feelings and an "I do."

Marriage, like our Christian faith, requires a firm, strong foundation. It also takes planning and preparation. That's where your beliefs and value system come into play. Knowing what you believe and value can have lasting positive effects on your marriage. Here's why: if you have similar beliefs and values, then you have a stronger foundation on which to build your marriage. Also, if you know your own beliefs and values as well as those of your future spouse, then you know your potential areas of strength and conflict.

By knowing where your strengths lie, you will have tools to face difficult times. You'll also enjoy knowing that on a very intimate level, you and your spouse's beliefs are essentially the same on important issues. You approach difficult decisions in a similar manner; you have the same viewpoint on issues like parenting, spending, or faith life.

Understanding where you and your spouse differ allows you to prepare for the challenges you'll face due to differing values and beliefs. Talking about your different views now may defuse later disagreements. It will give you the opportunity to plan for compromise ahead of time instead of in the midst of a difficult situation. And finally, discussing and dealing with how you differ in basic beliefs turns potential problems into strengths. Anytime you can face a challenge, talk about it, and deal with it in a healthy way, you strengthen your relationship.

For all these reasons, you will begin your marriage preparation journey with an exercise in self-discovery. You will define what values mean to you, determine your values, and discern the similarities and differences between your values and your spouse's values.

NOW LET'S GET TO WORK!

» What is a value?

what you live by

Importance

Criteria by which we make
decisions

» How can knowing your values be useful on a personal level?

Analyze situations + react
appropriately

» How can knowing your values be useful in relationships?

Come to shared decisions

SCENARIO ▶ Richard just finished college with his master's degree in business administration and is looking for the right career and a lasting relationship. He is an ambitious man who always tackles difficult situations with hard work and tenacity. He comes from a great family and is looking for a lifelong mate in order to start a family of his own. He is set up on many blind dates but finds that many of the women he meets seem superficial and interested in him because his degree suggests he has a promising future. He decides to wait to pursue a relationship until he finds a job and gets settled into the workforce. He interviews for an entry-level position at a computer programming company, but decides he could be more useful in a different environment. He is offered a job as a manager of a major corporation making an enormous salary, but he declines the job because it seems boring to him. Eventually, Richard decides to open his own company doing something he loves. It doesn't offer much money at first, but he loves being his own boss and seeing his plans come to fruition. Three months after his company begins turning a profit, he meets a young lady who is a bit shy and very intelligent. She has such a lovely spirit about her that Richard's friends and family immediately fall in love with her. He marries her within six months of their first date and they both work hard to have a strong, loving marriage.

Values worksheet

Love	Teamwork	Character	Opportunities
Fun	Tolerance	Importance	Self-Worth
Hope	Happiness	Genuineness	Support
Practicality	Intelligence	Truth	Harmony
Altruism	Spirituality	Community	Life
God	Creativity	Competition	Winning
Family	Relaxation	Financial Stability	Service
Friendship	Power	Understanding	Travel
Structure	Commitment	Confidence	Sacrifice
Success	Integrity	Self-Discipline	Wealth
Money	Dependence	Appearance	Self-Control
Relationships	Romance	Competence	Decisiveness
Education	Beauty	Stability	Trustworthiness
Work	Acceptance	Independence	Achievement
Routine	Religion	Excitement	Hard Work
Discipline	Adventure	Change	Communication
Career	Trust	Strength	Idealism
Faith	Loyalty	Courage	Assertiveness
Giving	Health	Dependability	Completion
Peace	Talent	Kindness	Opportunity
Respect	Consistency	Self-Reliance	Pragmatism
Devotion	Mercy	Chastity	Advancement
Recognition	Morality	Self-Sufficiency	Growth
Honesty	Passion	Justice	Unity
Risk-Taking	Belonging	Wisdom	Prosperity
Humility	Prayer	Organization	Enlightenment
Cooperation	Safety	Approval	Enrichment
Responsibility	Difference	Learning	Agreement
Freedom	Control	Compassion	Open-Mindedness
Simplicity	Predictability	Purpose	Ingenuity

MY VALUES

1. Relationships
2. Education
3. Work
4. Learning
5. Communication
6. Genuineness
7. Freedom
8. Humility
9. Teamwork
10. Character

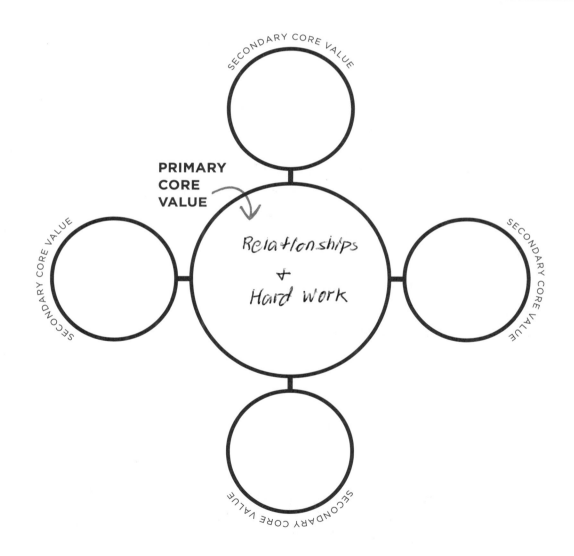

SECONDARY CORE VALUE

PRIMARY CORE VALUE

SECONDARY CORE VALUE

Relationships + Hard Work

SECONDARY CORE VALUE

SECONDARY CORE VALUE

My values in relationship

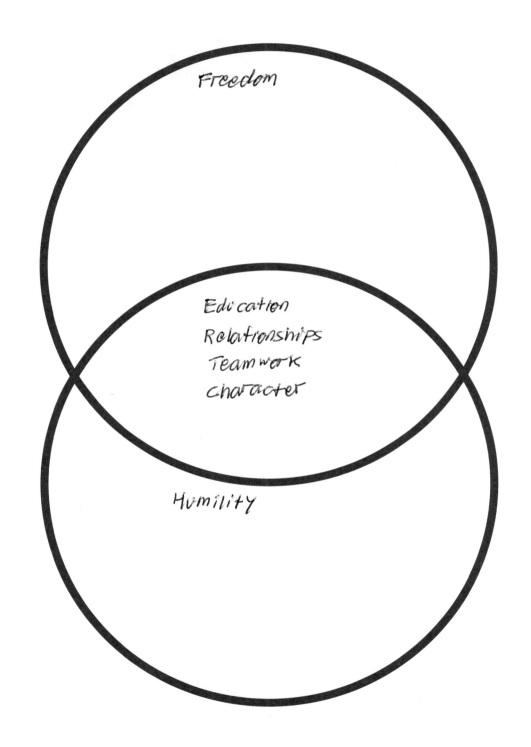

Freedom

Education
Relationships
Teamwork
Character

Humility

Communication

WHY COMMUNICATE? ✳ COMMUNICATION SKILLS

COMMUNICATION IN PRACTICE ✳ THE VIRTUE OF FORGIVENESS

Why communicate?

Most important of all, continue to show deep love for each other, for love makes up for many of your faults.

[1 PETER 4:8]

The National Center for Health Statistics claims that the number one reason cited as cause for divorce is lack of effective communication. Marital counseling often begins with teaching couples basic communication skills. Why? Well, no couple ever needed counseling because they were understood too well by their spouse. Usually, when things go wrong in a marriage, somehow something got warped in the communication process or suffered because of a lack of communication.

Everyone thinks they know how to communicate because they know how to talk. In marriage, simply knowing how to chat is not enough. We have to become conscious of how we say things, when we say things, how well we listen, and how well we understand what our spouse is attempting to convey.[12, 13]

Communication occurs both verbally and nonverbally. You communicate not just with words but with tone, gestures, and body language. How you say something is as important as what you say.[14] Being aware of how you and your spouse communicate on all levels is important to learning how to strengthen your relationship. By improving your communication skills, you'll find it easier to come to agreements and compromises in times of conflict. In addition, you may even be able to prevent conflict by simply communicating better.

The key is *listening* and attempting to understand. Again, no husband or wife has ever complained about being understood too thoroughly. By committing to listen actively to your spouse and to respect what he or she is trying to say and how he or she is feeling at any given moment, you are showing your spouse how much you value him.[12] Being heard is a great gift to give someone you love.

Real communication is not easy. It would be much easier to dictate or demand your needs and wants than to cooperate with another.[12] But a marriage won't last long under a dictator's regime. And your spouse may walk away from conversations with you bitter and angry.

Re-visit your relationship values. Where does communication fit into those values? Many marriage therapists place common beliefs and strong communication skills at the top of their list of the most essential components in a successful marriage.[15] How do you rank communication?

In this workshop, you learn basic communication skills and conflict resolution skills before you engage in the big topics of marriage. This is purposeful. Use these skills as you journey through this workbook. If you learn to communicate your expectations, beliefs, needs, wants, and desires clearly, you will maximize your time spent in marriage preparation. In addition, you will end this workshop with a greater, more thorough knowledge of your *spouse's* expectations, beliefs, needs, wants, and desires.

The **nearly-wed** game

Directions ▸ *Please answer the following questions on full-sized sheets of paper. Number the sheets of paper. Place one answer on each sheet of paper. For example, on Sheet 1, write the answer to Question 1. Continue until you have all 10 questions answered. Do not show your future spouse!*

1. Where was your first date? *Aquarium*

2. Where are you spending Christmas this year? *Matt's family*

3. How many children do you want to have? *4*

4. How many times a week will you have sex? *1-3*

5. What city/town will you live in? *Denver*

6. Who will be in charge of your finances? *Together*

7. How often and where will you go to church? *1/week*

8. How do you define infidelity or unfaithfulness? *Emotional, physical, mental cheating*

9. What is your idea of a good "date night"? *out to dinner, movie, walking*

10. What is the maximum amount of money you can spend without having to consult your spouse? *$5K*

Communication skills

TRY TO
Talk when calm...ask for time if you are too upset to be rational
Be aware of your intention for confronting the issue
Use "I" statements: I feel like...; I think...; When this happens I need...
Empathize and understand where the other person is coming from
Maintain eye contact
Use open body language
Be aware of facial expressions
Be aware of how your body is positioned
Do not interrupt
Listen
Restate what the other person has said before responding
Summarize what you heard the other person say and how you think the other person feels
Listen again
Take time to think before you respond
Use specific examples, not generalizations

TRY TO AVOID
Name calling
Win/lose situations
Accusatory "you" statements
Blame
Preaching
Becoming silent
Bringing up the past
Comparing spouse to past relationships
Comparing spouse to members of his/her family
Arguing in public
Exaggerating
Ultimatums
Embarrassing your spouse
Using "never" or "always"
Patronizing
Pride
Tuning out
Walking out
Sarcasm
Profane language
Yelling

If you always restate or summarize what someone has said before you respond, you significantly reduce the chance of misunderstandings. When your partner is allowed to clarify any unclear issues before you answer, then **you are more likely to address the issues that need addressing** instead of the issues you think need addressing.

A soft answer turneth away wrath: but grievous words stir up anger. [PROVERBS 15:1]

Feeling words for communication

Angry
Used
Overwhelmed
Furious
Nervous
Annoyed
Upset
Tired
Sad
Elated
Anxious
Miserable
Ecstatic
Content
Frustrated
Ticked off
Pleased
Distressed
Worried
Excited
Afraid
Depressed
Fortunate
Cheerful
Hurt
Fearful
Irritated
Scared
Irate
Foolish
Happy
Outraged
Unloved
Lost
Calm
Disappointed

» Potential stressors in marriage

CoviD
Money
Family Obligations
Children

You *will* disagree
...**now what?**

19

Communication in practice

❯❯ Let's talk about

Husband should be
more considerate

Problem solving model

- Identify the issue at hand
- Brainstorm solutions
- Evaluate which solutions may work for you
- Decide on a solution
- Commit to a solution

✗ Do not fill out

CONFLICT MANAGEMENT PRACTICE [14]

1 I feel _____ (name the feeling)
when you _____
(name the behavior).

2 Maybe I could have _____
_____ (take some responsibility
for the conflict and state what you could have done to make it better).

3 Let's try to _____
_____. **OR What can we do in the future when faced with this?** _____
_____.

20

The virtue of forgiveness

Forgiveness is a loving, freeing, and graceful act. But often, it is a bitter pill to swallow. To forgive is to give a gift to yourself and to another person, someone who may or may not deserve forgiveness. The magic of forgiveness is not in changing another's behavior, but it is in seeing your behavior change by shedding the shackles of hurt, anger, and resentment. It is very difficult to look at your spouse in terms of forever and always when yesterday's battles are still ringing in your ears.

Forgiveness is a *choice*, not a *feeling*. It is a choice couples make every day to let go of hurts, disagreements, slights, or harsh words. It is pushing pride aside and burying the idea that you must be right. Without this daily choice, this daily decision, couples quickly get bogged down in bitter disagreements and rehashing the past.

> Christ's mercy cannot penetrate our hearts if we have not forgiven those who sinned against us. **Love is indivisible.** We cannot love God (whom we cannot see) and not love others (whom we do see). By refusing to forgive others, our hearts become hardened to God's mercy. However, confessing our sins opens us to God's grace.
> [**CATECHISM 2840**]

The challenges of forgiveness are when to forgive and how to forgive. Choose to be the first to say, "I'm sorry." A marriage is more important than pride, being right, or pretending nothing is wrong. Also, forgive by taking responsibility for your part in the issue. If what you said or did hurt your partner, but you feel you acted righteously, at least ask forgiveness for hurting the one you love.

Once given freely, a couple has to let go of the issue and move on. The same old anger and hurt cannot be reused and recycled once forgiven. By letting go and moving on, a couple gives their marriage new life and a second chance.

POINTS TO PONDER

"We forgive freely or we do not really forgive at all."
— LEWIS B. SMEDES

....

"Without deep humility, true forgiveness is impossible...and will never happen."
— MARTHA KILPATRICK

....

"There is no point in burying a hatchet if you're going to put up a marker on the site."
— SYDNEY HARRIS

....

"Forgiveness is me giving up my right to hurt you for hurting me." — ANONYMOUS

....

"One forgives to the degree that one loves." — FRANÇOIS DE LA ROCHEFOUCAULD

....

"Don't let the sun go down on your anger."
— EPHESIANS 4:26

....

"Forgive us our trespasses, as we forgive those who trespass against us." — MATTHEW 6:12

Conversations

FAITH AND SPIRITUALITY ✳ FAMILY OF ORIGIN

COHABITATION ✳ CHILDREN ✳ CAREER ✳ FINANCES

INTIMACY ✳ COMMITMENT

Faith and spirituality

What is faith? What is a sacrament? When it comes to God, what do you believe? What does your spouse believe? Do you share a common religion? Where will you go to church? Where will your future children go to church? Where does God fit into your values?

These are all questions you will want to address before your wedding. Know what you and your spouse believe. Know what the Bible and the Church teach about marriage.

Christian marriages are covenants between spouses and between the couple and God. A covenant is a biblical word for contract. The most important part of this union, however, is not its contractual nature, but its sacramental nature. The Catholic Church teaches that a valid marriage between two baptized Christians is a sacrament. The most amazing thing about the sacrament of marriage is that, unlike other sacraments that bestow a moment of grace, marriage bestows an ongoing, daily grace. Grace doesn't just spill down in an instant of forgiveness, as in reconciliation, but flows constantly in marriage to saturate every aspect of life.

> The Christian Family is the first place of education in prayer. Based on the sacrament of Marriage, **the family is the "domestic church"** where God's children learn to pray "as the Church" and to persevere in prayer.
> [**CATECHISM 2685**]

The fact that marriage is a sacrament is very important in times of marital stress. Keep in mind that grace is a constant state in marriage. When you and your spouse are at odds because of differences, disagreements, or fighting, partake in other sacraments, such as the Eucharist or reconciliation. The grace of these sacraments will act as a booster shot of grace in your relationship. It is grace that helps you with forgiveness of self and spouse, that helps with finding peace in marriage, that helps with staying focused on and committed to God and each other.

The practice of faith and spirituality is strongly rooted in many families and relationships. The way your family of origin worshipped may have a strong impact on your expectations of faith for yourself, your spouse, and your future family. Because of this, it is very important to learn about each other's religious convictions and the strength of those convictions before the "I do's."

Talk to each other. Communicate. Knowing about your spouse's relationship with God is too important to leave to a later date. Share your expectations for the role faith and religion will have in your marriage and in parenting. Come to some decisions beforehand so that your children will not be born into a religious minefield.

You and your spouse may have different beliefs and religions. Use this time to learn about one another...ask questions, visit each other's churches, and pray together. Attend classes, speak with teachers in each of your faiths, and read books. Merge your prayers and religious traditions so that both of your beliefs are honored.

Coming together to learn about each other's experience of faith, even if your religions are the same, can be a wonderful way to strengthen your relationship. And remember, marriage is not simply a legal undertaking, but a commitment to each other and to God that symbolizes Christ's commitment to us. Hence, the "until death do us part..." section of the vows.

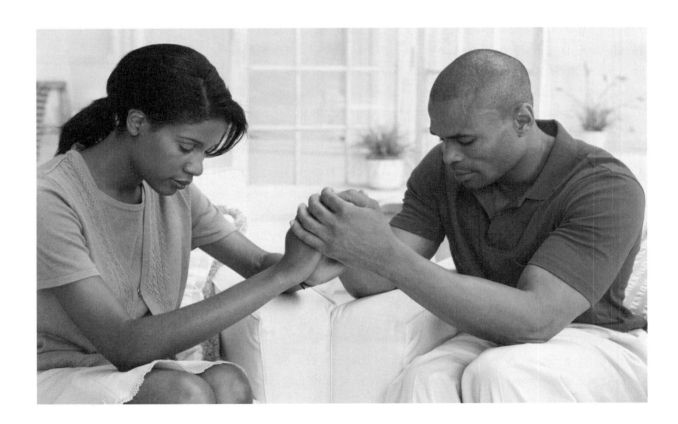

The faith banner

SPIRITUAL LIFE	**CHILDREN**
Pray together	4 children 1-3 years after marriage
COHABITATION — own a house or two Live in Colorado	**CAREER** — One day practice together
FINANCES — Shared Finances	**INTIMACY** — Spicy sex life
COMMITMENT — Till death do us part + we'll find each other in heaven	**FAMILY OF ORIGIN** — understand that both of our families are different + that's okay they have different way of expressing love

THE **PAL** METHOD OF PRAYER

PRAISE
ASK
LISTEN

PRAISE *Through him let us continually offer up a sacrifice of praise to God, that is, the fruit of lips that acknowledge his name.*

[**HEBREWS 13:15**]

ASK *Therefore I tell you, whatever you ask in prayer, believe that you have received it, and it will be yours.*

[**MARK 11:24**]

LISTEN *Behold, I stand at the door and knock. If anyone hears my voice and opens the door, I will come in to him and eat with him, and he with me.*

[**REVELATION 3:20**]

If you have never prayed together before, and would like to begin, start with baby steps.

- Say grace before meals together.
- Say a prayer (The Lord's Prayer, etc.) before a long journey.
- Read a Bible verse or a devotional with your spouse each night.
- Go to church weekly.
- Seek out resources within your church community. Attend prayer meetings, Bible studies, penance services, or any other program for couples and families.

> In virtue of the sacrament of Marriage, by which they signify and share the mystery of the unity and faithful love between Christ and the Church, **Christian married couples help one another to attain holiness** in their married life and in the rearing of their children. [**LG, #11**] [18]

Conversation starters

Describe your relationship with God. How do you nourish your relationship with God?

Where does God fit into your values in everyday life?

If your commitment to your faith, your church, or your religion differs from that of your spouse, how does this affect your relationship with each other?

How can you merge both of your practices of faith and spirituality in your marriage?

If God is not in your core values individually or as a couple, what makes you seek marriage in the Catholic Church?

Marriage is a sacrament. What does this mean to you?

Family of origin

Everyone has a family history. Our past and the way each of us was raised affect the way we approach marriage and the manner in which we handle marital difficulties and successes. You must explore your family history, how you were raised, and the role of your family of origin in your wedded life to understand how your family of origin impacts your marriage.

Some of you may think, "I want a marriage just like my parents," or, "I want to raise my family exactly like I was raised." Many couples approaching marriage have wonderful role models in one or both of their family of origin's relationship. From childhood experience, people can learn the true meaning of fidelity, mutual support, spiritual nurturing, love, trust, obedience, and faith.

Unfortunately, that is not true for all couples. Some people have lived through homes plagued with addiction, violence, poverty, instability, abuse, apostasy, neglect, or psychological control. For those who have had a less stable upbringing, marriage can seem both a daunting task and a chance to get it right.

Making marriage work cannot be a knee-jerk reaction to upbringing. In other words, doing exactly the same or exactly the opposite of how you were raised is not the answer for your marriage. Your marital challenge lies in making choices based on creating a strong foundation for marriage rather than making choices in reaction to personal history.

Couples always ask why children of divorce have a greater chance of divorce themselves. Often, it's because children of divorce think that by saying they will not be like their parents, that alone ensures marital success. Children of divorce usually know what *not* to do in marriage, but because they have not experienced a successful marriage, they often do not know what it is they *should* do.

To create a strong, stable foundation for marriage, all couples must work together to seek and find common ground. Begin by discovering and living by common values. Work together or with a professional to determine what effect your family of origin has on your communication skills, your ability to manage conflict, your spending practices, your approach to parenting, your ability to commit, your understanding of intimacy, and your personal and marital relationship with God. Everyone hoping to learn from their past must do so by being conscious of the effects of that past and conscious of the changes they need to make together, as a couple. Then they must devise a plan and rely on the support of stable people in their lives.

For many, your family of origin continues to be a part of your everyday life. How do you feel about your future in-laws? Your relationship with your future spouse's family will greatly impact your marriage and the family you create. Before your marriage, consider how you will relate to each other's family of origin, what boundaries you will have, and the role you want your in-laws to take in your new life together.

From every standpoint, your family of origin has shaped who you are and the type of marriage you want to have. By working together as a couple, you consciously can make the choices necessary for creating the best atmosphere for a strong and committed marriage.

But from everlasting to everlasting the Lord's Love is with those who fear him, and his righteousness with his children's children...

[**PSALM 103:17**]

28

Deal

Directions ▶ *In this exercise, you will examine the influence of your family of origin on your future married life. Please answer the following questions on index cards. Number the cards. Place one answer on each card. For example, on Card 1, write the answer to Question 1. Continue until you have all 6 questions answered. Do not show your future spouse!*

1. Who made the major decisions in your household growing up? *Both*

2. How did your family handle disagreements growing up? *Dad usually right Mom executive decisions*

3. Who handled the majority of chores in your home? *Mom cook. Dad chores kids chores*

4. How many hours of work did the primary breadwinner put in per week? *80-90 30*

5. How were you disciplined growing up? *Disappointed in you*

6. How was love shown in your house? *Openly Acts of service*

Conversation starters

What are the three most significant events in your past that have shaped you into who you are today?

In relation to family, what is the one thing in your past you never want to repeat?

What is the one thing in your past you hope to share in your marriage?

How involved will your family of origin be in your marriage?

In what ways can your family of origin support you in your marriage?

In what ways will your family of origin be a challenge for you?

When you hear the phrase, "You don't just marry a person, you marry his/her family as well," what reaction do you have?

Cohabitation

Cohabitation tends to be a controversial subject for many couples contemplating marriage. Few are aware of exactly what the Church teaches until they approach a priest about their intent to marry. The Catholic Church does not condone cohabitation prior to marriage for several reasons. First and foremost is that cohabiting couples divorce at higher rates than couples who do not cohabit, and report less satisfaction with marriage.[3, 5, 6, 7, 10, 16, 19] And if you consider that 50% of marriages fail, a chance greater than 50% is not an encouraging statistic. Second, the Bible speaks repeatedly about the sinfulness of having sex outside of marriage, and cohabitation is the equivalent of outwardly flaunting a blatant disregard for this teaching.

The Catholic Church did not make up the rule that couples should not live together before marriage. This precedent was set by Jesus' teachings on chastity, marriage, and love throughout the Bible. Regardless of your opinion or your conscience or your gut feeling, God does not contradict His teachings and laws by sending us personal mixed messages. One of the reasons couples most often cite for living together is to ensure marital success. Couples claim a trial run at marriage will help them to avoid divorce and confirm compatibility. On the surface, this sounds responsible, even smart. But one cannot trial-run marriage when you consider that living together is neither a sacrament nor a covenant. Marriage is defined as both. When neither God nor a contract is present in a relationship, that relationship can never be the equivalent of marriage.

Regardless of the statistics, biblical truth, or logical reasoning, many people live together prior to getting married. Our Church recognizes this reality and issues a challenge to you, the bride and groom. Separate. Make arrangements to live separately from now until your wedding day. While there are several long-term downsides to living together, there are no long-term downsides to living apart until your wedding day. In a relationship blessed by God, this time apart will only solidify your decision to marry.

cohabitation
\ko-,ha-be-'ta-shen\
noun 1. to live together as if a married couple.

Below are positive benefits of living apart before marriage

- Strengthen your friendship.

- Achieve greater intimacy by working on other areas of intimacy besides sex.

- Work on communication and conflict resolution.

- Use the space granted by living apart to give perspective for stronger, more reliable decision making.

- Give your marriage a greater chance for success.

Conversation starters

Once you are legally and
sacramentally joined,
what expectations do you
have for living together
as a married couple?

For those living together,
what is preventing you from
living apart until your wedding day?

What are your greatest
fears about living together?

What do you look forward
to when living together as
husband and wife?

cohabitation
\ko-,ha-be-'ta-shen\
noun 2. to live together or in company.

So you're getting a roommate. Now what? Your focus up to this point has been on all the hurdles of planning a wedding. You even may have been talking about all the big issues of marriage itself: finances, children, values, and beliefs. But have you considered the logistics of living together?

Many fights start with toothpaste in the sink or dirty laundry on the floor. Who wants to waste time fighting over pet peeves when there are so many bigger issues at stake? But it happens. So take a minute, laugh a little, and learn just what straw may break the camel's back in your marriage.

House rules

BEDROOM
No eating
No shoes
No TV

BATHROOM
Don't spit on mirror

KITCHEN / DINING ROOM
Vater in dirty dishes

LIVING ROOM / DEN
only meg does laundry

YARD

32

Children

In marriage, you are called to procreation if you are biologically capable. Having a child is the greatest gift and the greatest challenge you will experience as husband and wife. It is life-changing in so many ways. While you can never truly prepare for the changes a child will bring to your life and your relationship, you can reach some agreements ahead of time in regard to certain aspects of parenting.

Parenting children can be one of the most stressful responsibilities in a marriage if you are not on the same page. And even if you are, it's still tough.

> The conjugal community is established upon the consent of the spouses. **Marriage and the family** are ordered to the good of the spouses and to procreation and education of children.
> [CATECHISM 2201]

Have the big conversations now. Recognize how your family of origin affects how you view parenting. Talk about theories of discipline. Be aware that your values affect your concept of parenting. If you have similar values, parenting on the same page becomes just a little bit easier.

Keep in mind, also, that common beliefs can be extremely reassuring if you face unexpected pregnancy or infertility. While nothing can truly prepare you for either of these events, a strong marriage is your greatest source of comfort.

Conversation starters

How many children do you want?

If there are stepchildren involved, how will you deal with parenting issues?

How long will you wait before having children?

How will you deal with unexpected pregnancy?

How will you deal with infertility?

How will you plan pregnancies?

How do you want to discipline your children?

Will one of you be a stay-at-home parent? How will you make that work?

In case of infertility, would you consider adoption or foster children?

Have you considered how you will handle sick or challenged children?

What are potential benefits of babysitting regularly together?

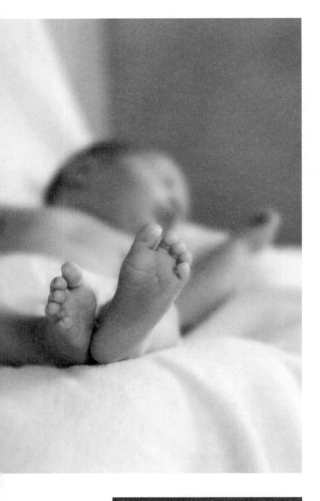

Natural family planning

Many couples choosing to marry neglect to consider how they want to plan their families, both the number of children they want to have and the spacing between their children. Even when couples discuss this, many are unaware of the alternatives to traditional "birth control" methods.

Natural Family Planning is the Catholic Church's answer to a couple's moral obligation to recognize the sexual act as a source of unity and procreation in marriage. Because traditional birth control methods interfere with a person's fertility, which is a gift from God, couples must consider how to work with fertility rather than fight against it.

Pope Paul VI shed light on this subject in *Humanae Vitae*, putting to rest misunderstandings in Church teachings. In a nutshell, he wrote that sex in marriage is a good thing, as close as you can get to the life-giving character of God Himself. He encourages couples to see sex as intimacy, unity, and a strengthening of marriage. In marriage, couples should be best friends, sexual partners, and one heart and one soul...truly "one flesh."

By advocating NFP as the only choice for family planning, the Church wants to support and strengthen the marriage. Our faith teaches us to love each other, to work hard at nurturing intimacy in marriage, and to truly see our spouse as the gift God intends him or her to be. NFP supports all these things and is the only method that respects God's intent for sex and love within marriage.

The Benefits of NFP

1 NFP requires couples to have an intimate understanding of the woman's body and the woman's cycle of fertility. So whether a couple is committed to preventing pregnancy or achieving it, NFP can assist in both. No other method of birth control can do that.

2 NFP prevents spouses from taking intimacy for granted. Spouses are forced to communicate continually and, when avoiding pregnancy, find other ways of achieving intimacy on the days

A child is not something owed to one, but a gift. The "supreme gift of marriage" is a human person. A child may not be considered a piece of property, an idea to which an alleged "right to a child" would lead.

[**CATECHISM 2378**]

when the sexual act can cause conception.

3 For couples who use NFP, women are reported to be appreciative of their husband's desire to understand their bodies instead of expecting them to deal with fertility alone. In addition, wives value that their husbands choose to exert self-control and sacrifice pleasure for the sake of their common values and stance on pregnancy.

4 NFP is not birth control but "responsible parenting," which the Church stresses is the responsibility of the husband and wife in the marriage relationship. Responsible parenting is the recognition of the social, psychological, physical, and economic reality of a couple, which leads to their decision to have a child (or more children) or put off pregnancy for a period of time. (Remember, no couple can legitimately go into a Catholic marriage with a determination to have no children.)

5 There are no side effects, as in hormonal methods of birth control.

6 It's free.

THE MYTHS ABOUT NFP AND THE CHURCH'S TEACHINGS ON SEX IN MARRIAGE

MYTH: **The Church wants all couples to have large families.**

TRUTH *The Church teaches "responsible parenting." Couples must carefully weigh their obligations to God, to their spouse, to existing children, and to other responsibilities in order to decide the spacing of and the number of their children.*

MYTH: **The Church teaches that sex is for procreation only.**

TRUTH *The Church recognizes that sex is not only for procreation, but for strengthening marriage as well. Research supports that married couples have greater sexual satisfaction than couples who are unmarried. Truly, the Church wants married couples to have sex, and enjoy it!*

MYTH: **NFP is the "pull out" method.**

TRUTH *NFP is NOT the "pull out" method (the withdrawal of the penis prior to ejaculation). NFP is a scientific understanding of the fertility of a woman's body. It includes learning about a woman's ovulatory cycle, including secretions and temperature changes, to name a few. NFP requires a couple to communicate and work together to log a woman's cycle in order to know when having sex can cause pregnancy.*

MYTH: **NFP is ineffective as birth control.**

TRUTH *NFP has proven to be approximately 99% effective when couples follow the rules of the method. Learning NFP takes a little reading and/or training, but once learned becomes a healthy, safe habit in a marriage. In addition, there are no side effects from hormones. There is no reduction in sensation from barrier methods. And there are no sponges, rings, shots, or diaphragms to consider.*

Career

We spend the majority of every day at work. Often, we see our coworkers more than our spouse during the work week. Yet we don't always discuss the impact our job has on our marriage.

Having income is necessary in order to live. But exactly how much income is enough? When children are born, are two incomes necessary? How will you balance family and career? How will you prioritize family life and work life? You've deciphered your values for your relationship. Now, how will you apply them to your career?

The hardest thing for some couples is deciding what income is necessary for living and what is to fulfill wants rather than needs. Where do the emotional needs of your marriage and family fit into your desire for financial stability, wealth, or material goods?

We are bombarded with the media's version of what we need to be happy: vacations, media equipment, dining out, new cars. Yet, are these needs or wants? Consider what you would do to streamline your lifestyle if one of you lost your job or if one of your careers was in serious conflict with the values in your marriage.

What if your job *does* cause conflict? Maybe you work extra hours and travel often. Maybe you work in close proximity to members of the opposite sex. Possibly you cannot share the details of your work, or your spouse doesn't agree with your career choice. How will you handle the discord that arises from these issues?

Many couples have no choice but to both work just to survive. In that case, you have to be even more aware of the need to nurture your marriage and find time for your family. You are challenged with balancing your job with your desire for a strong marriage.

When considering the importance of your career in your marriage, keep in mind some variables. You may have children or family members to care for. You may or may not need a double income. One of you may not be as invested in his or her career as the other. You may have the option of part-time work. Your children's caretakers should share your values and discipline beliefs. These are all tough issues that have to be taken into account when discussing your career in connection with your marriage.

> Human work proceeds directly from persons created in the image of God and called to prolong the work of creation by subduing the earth, both with and for one another. Hence work is a duty. **Work honors the Creator's gifts** and the talents received from Him.
> [CATECHISM 2427]

Commit to the Lord whatever you do, and your plans will succeed.
[PROVERBS 16:3]

Balance

1 Agree on acceptable amounts of overtime or travel time.

2 Consider changing jobs if your marriage is at stake.

3 To stay connected, talk to your spouse about your job.

4 Discuss what outside activities to participate in and which ones are unnecessary.

5 If you are able, hire someone for cleaning or yard work so that you can spend more time with family.

6 Take time out to create memorable experiences for your family, even if it's just a weekly Game Night.

Whatever your hand finds to do, do it with all your might.

[ECCLESIASTES 9:10]

TAKING RESPONSIBILITY

	% HUSBAND	% WIFE
Who handles housework?	50	50
Whose career takes priority?	50	50
Who will take off work to care for sick kids or family members?	50	50
If it's an option, who will stay home once children are born?	50	50

Conversation starters

Will the person with the higher income have more say in spending and budgeting? Discuss.

Address what changes you can make to your workload in order to tackle debt.

What expectations do you have in regards to income needs, parenting, household tasks, and teamwork?

Finances

Finances are often blamed for a majority of divorces. However, the culprit in divorce is less financial than a lack of clear communication about finances.

When a couple clearly *understands* their financial picture, *agrees* how to handle their finances, and *has a plan* in place to prepare for the future, that couple is less likely to encounter conflict. Therefore, you must have a thorough understanding of your finances prior to marriage. Not only should you be aware of each other's current income and debt, but you should also come to an agreement about how you will handle your debts and allocate your income once married.

Matthew 6:21 says, "For where your treasure is, there your heart will be also." If you want to truly have a clear picture of your values (your heart), take a close look at your spending (your treasure). Spending habits are one of the most black-and-white reflections of a person's values. People pay for what they value most...whether shoes or movies, boats or donations, vacations or education. As a couple, you will need to look at your expenditures to know what each of you spends money on and decide how you feel about the values you see expressed in your spending.

On this page, you will notice a snapshot of your current financial picture. On the following pages, you will discover a basic budget worksheet that can fit a variety of lifestyles. Note that tithing, or donations, tops the list of expenditures in the budget. What does putting charity first mean to you?

Take time to fill out these worksheets together. And when you do, remember that communication about finances is the best way to avoid the kind of arguments and fights that lead to marriage failure.

My financial snapshot

INCOME

1. $ *Practice Income*
2. $_____
3. $_____
4. $_____

MY CURRENT INCOME

DEBT

1. $ *Student Loans*
2. $ *Practice Loan*
3. $_____
4. $_____

MY CURRENT DEBT

OUR FINANCIAL HABITS

How many credit cards do you have?	2 + 2
Who is the bigger spender?	Meg
Will you have joint or separate checking accounts?	Joint
Who will pay the bills?	Joint
Who has the most debt?	Meg
How many credit cards will you have once married?	4 - 6
Who is the bigger saver?	Matt
Who is in charge of your finances?	Joint
How much do you spend on dining out per week?	$100 - $150
Who is most committed to debt reduction?	Matt

Our financial future

- Children's college fund(s)
- Retirement
- Life insurance
- Paying off debt
- Savings (rainy day, Christmas, etc.)
- Disability insurance

Budget worksheet

INCOME	
Income 1:	
Income 2:	
Income 3:	
INCOME TOTALS ▶	

EXPENSES	

Donations	
Charity	
Religious Organizations	
DONATIONS TOTALS ▶	

Home	
Mortgage / rent	
Utilities	
Home telephone	
Cell phone	
Home repairs / improvement	
Home security	
Cable TV	
Internet service	
Yard / garden care	
HOME TOTALS ▶	

Daily Living	
Groceries	
Child care / tuition	
Dry cleaning	
Housecleaning service	
DAILY LIVING TOTALS ▶	

Transportation	
Car payment	
Gas / fuel	
Car insurance	
Repairs / oil changes	
Car wash / detailing services	
Parking	
Public transportation	
TRANSPORTATION TOTALS ▶	

Entertainment	
Video rentals / music / books	
Movies / plays / concerts	
Clubs / bars / restaurants	
ENTERTAINMENT TOTALS ▶	

Health	
Health insurance	
Prescription / over-the-counter medications	
Co-payments / out-of-pocket	
Disability insurance	
HEALTH TOTALS ▶	

Vacations / Recreation	
Transportation	
Accommodations	
Food	
Souvenirs	
Pet boarding	
Gym / team dues	
Sports equipment	
VACATION / RECREATION TOTALS ▶	

Dues / Subscriptions	
Magazines / newspapers	
Professional organizations	
DUES / SUBSCRIPTION TOTALS ▶	

Personal	
Clothing	
Gifts	
Salon / barber	
PERSONAL TOTALS ▶	

Financial Obligations	
Long-term savings	
Term life insurance	
Retirement (401k, Roth IRA)	
Debt reduction	
Income tax (additional)	
Other obligations	
FINANCIAL OBLIGATION TOTALS ▶	

Miscellaneous Payments	
College fund(s):	
Other:	
MISC. PAYMENTS TOTALS ▶	

TOTAL EXPENSES ▶

CASH SHORT / EXTRA *(TOTAL INCOME - TOTAL EXPENSES)* ▶

Intimacy

When we think of intimacy in marriage, we think of sex. Sex is an important part of the marital relationship and is the physical consecration of the marriage bond. But intimacy refers to so much more than just your sexual relationship. The Encarta Dictionary defines intimacy as a "close personal relationship" and "a detailed knowledge resulting from a close or long association."

Intimacy can be as small as touching your spouse on the shoulder as you go by or as private as the sexual act itself. Intimacy is both romance and quiet glances. No part of your intimate relationship can be ignored without creating some level of dissatisfaction in the marriage bond.

There are three main types of intimacy that must be nurtured in your marriage: emotional, physical, and spiritual intimacy. Emotional intimacy refers to loving words, talking, romance, confiding in each other, kindness, friendship, gestures, and unspoken communication. Physical intimacy refers to touch, foreplay, affection, and sex. Spiritual intimacy involves inviting God into the deepest parts of your marriage. If you ignore one of these areas, the other areas will suffer.

Emotional and physical intimacy can be best summarized in the following manner: *Say* "I love you" as often as you can. *Show* "I love you" even more.

To experience intimacy on a profoundly spiritual level, we must commit to selflessness. Selflessness is often described in religious language as a dying to self. This means that your needs, wants, and desires are subordinate to those of your spouse. This does not mean you become your spouse's slave or a doormat. It simply means that if you put your spouse first and your spouse puts you first, then both of you are being treated as a precious gift to each other. Both of your needs are being met by the other, not by your own hand. This creates true intimacy because you are entrusting another person to care for you, and by putting your spouse first you become fulfilled and affirmed in your relationship.

It is difficult to experience this type of intimacy without trust at the center of your marriage. Your trust in God, your trust in your

> Sexuality is ordered to the conjugal love of man and woman. In marriage the physical intimacy of the spouses becomes **a sign and pledge of spiritual communion**.
> [CATECHISM 2360]

spouse, your trust in yourself, your trust in your decision to marry your partner, and your trust in the sacrament of marriage have to be heartfelt and authentic. Having true intimacy in your marriage depends on it.

Do you feel loved when your spouse...

1. Buys you gifts or takes you for an evening out?

2. Shows affection?

3. Tells you how wonderful or attractive you are?

4. Helps you with household chores or yard work?

5. Takes time to talk with you and really listen?

6. Shows appreciation for all you do?

♥ **I FEEL LOVED WHEN MY SPOUSE...**

performs acts of service

♥ **MY SPOUSE FEELS LOVE WHEN I...**

spend quality time

Going out or staying in?

Meg Going Out	Matt staying In
Movie Theater	streaming services
Dinner out	Cooking Dinner

44

Roadblocks to intimacy

- Pornography
- Masturbation
- Internet relationships
- Anger
- Addictions
- Infidelity
- Confiding in others instead of spouse
- Poor communication
- Secrets
- Selfishness
- Unwilling to forgive
- Rejecting God's role in your marriage

Let marriage be held in honor among all, and let the marriage bed be undefiled for God will judge the sexually immoral and adulterous.

[HEBREWS 13:4]

Conversation starters

Are sexual relations of primary importance in your relationship at this time? In what way?

Have you shared your sexual history with your spouse? If not, why not?

What are some of your reservations about sex in your marriage?

How do you anticipate marriage affecting your views on sex in your relationship?

What sexual expectations do you have of your partner in marriage? Share them.

If you have committed to abstinence in your courtship, how do you anticipate sex affecting your relationship?

ABSTINENCE PLEDGE

We, _____*Meg*_____ and _____*Matt*_____ ,
commit to God and to ourselves that, from this day until our wedding day, we will abstain from
sexual relations and rely on God's grace and our commitment to one another.

Commitment

You have probably heard the saying, "A wedding is a day, a marriage is a lifetime" (Catholic Engaged Encounter). While preparing for a wedding is often a necessary part of the journey to marriage, don't let it blind you to the seriousness of the commitment you are about to make.

A young woman, happily married many years and with four children, once said, "Some days we live on love; most days we live on commitment." She didn't mean it as a joke. Love is essential, but commitment is the foundation that allows love to flourish through hard times, anger, sorrow, or trauma.

> It can seem difficult, even impossible, to bind oneself for life to another human being. This makes it all the more important to proclaim the Good News that God loves us with a definitive and irrevocable love, that married couples share in this love, that it supports and sustains them, and that **by their own faithfulness they can be witnesses to God's faithful love.**
> [CATECHISM 1648]

Make no mistake. Real, lasting love is not merely a feeling. It is a decision every day to be loving, to forgive, to sacrifice, and to make marriage work. Marriage is a decision to stay when leaving appears easier, to work harder when quitting becomes tempting, and to give when taking seems justified.

Commitment in marriage is not just to stay married "until death do you part." It's also about committing to do the everyday things that keep a marriage healthy: helping with dishes, praying together, supporting each other's parenting styles. When we show commitment in these little things, we communicate to our partner how committed we are to the marriage itself.

What do you value about your spouse? What do you value about your relationship? Make a commitment to nurture your relationship by talking about those things you value most. And let your spouse know that no matter how tough it gets, you aren't going anywhere. There is no "Get Out of Jail FREE" card in a marriage. Marriage is for life. And commitment is your key to living "happily ever after."

When times are tough...

When the reality of marriage is overwhelming or difficult, you must commit to finding help. Sometimes you must swallow your pride and seek outside resources to make your marriage happier, fuller, and more peaceful. When faced with challenges that threaten the foundation of your marriage, commit to trying one of the following:

- Pastoral or professional counseling
- Books on marriage
- Working with a mentor couple
- Couple and/or individual retreats
- Journaling
- Adoration
- Prayer and fasting

Commitment is the last conversation for a reason. It is the glue that binds every issue discussed, every skill learned, and the very idea of marriage. But commitment is nothing if it is not defined by you and for your own relationship. What are you committing to? To whom are you committing? What does this mean to you? What does this mean to your life? Is God the center of your marriage?

This exercise requires you to evaluate your knowledge of yourself and your values, the skills you have learned, and the issues you have addressed in this workshop. Refer to your first exercise, when you shared why you wanted to marry your partner and what made him or her the right spouse for you. Then, with all this in mind, write a letter that, combined with your spouse's letter, will be a description of a strong foundation upon which to build your marriage.

Remember, this is a commitment love letter, one that describes your specific commitment to your spouse. Your experience of the day and your relationship is like no one else's. Therefore, your letter will be like no one else's.

My Commitment Love Letter

Dear _____ ,

_____

_____

_____

_____

_____

_____

_____

_____

_____

_____

_____

_____

_____

_____

_____

_____

_____

_____

Love,

_____

Challenge

MARRIAGE CHALLENGE PRAYER ✳ SUMMARY OF EXPERIENCE

A marriage challenge prayer

Dear Lord,

Thank you for the gift of marriage.
As we approach the altar, I challenge
myself to think less about the wedding
and more about our commitment to You
and each other. I challenge myself to
consider my spouse's values and feelings
instead of just my own. I challenge
myself to face our differences responsibly
and face our similarities lovingly. I
challenge myself to do Your will daily
in our marriage. Finally, I challenge
myself to put You at the center of all
the decisions that a wedding day and a
lifetime of marriage entail. Amen.

> The love of the spouses requires, of its very nature, the unity and indissolubility of the spouses' community of persons, which embraces their entire life...They are called to grow continually in their communion through day-to-day fidelity to their marriage promise of total mutual self-giving... It is deepened by lives of the common faith and by the Eucharist received together.
> [CATECHISM 1644]

Summary of experience

Take a moment to consider your personal perceptions of this workshop. Think about each chapter and consider which themes applied to you and your relationship.

Below, discuss areas of strength, weakness, and concern for each topic heading. Consider possible strategies for maximizing your strengths and working on your areas of weakness.

This exercise is a means to review what you have learned, tailor the workshop's outcomes to your needs, and provide a tangible synopsis of your experience for later reference or for use in further counsel.

CHOICE	
What did I learn about my relationship?	**What concerns do I have?**

CORE		
What did I learn about myself?	**What did I learn about my spouse?**	**What concerns do I have?**

COMMUNICATION

AS AN INDIVIDUAL...	AS A COUPLE...	
What are my strengths?	**What are our strengths?**	**What are areas of concern?**
What are my weaknesses?	**What are our weaknesses?**	

FAITH AND SPIRITUALITY

What are our strengths?	**What are our weaknesses?**	**What are areas of concern?**

FAMILY OF ORIGIN

What are our strengths?	**What are our weaknesses?**	**What are areas of concern?**

COHABITATION

What are our strengths?	What are our weaknesses?	What are areas of concern?

CHILDREN

What are our strengths?	What are our weaknesses?	What are areas of concern?

CAREER

What are our strengths?	What are our weaknesses?	What are areas of concern?

FINANCES

What are our strengths?	What are our weaknesses?	What are areas of concern?

INTIMACY

What are our strengths?	What are our weaknesses?	What are areas of concern?

COMMITMENT

What are our strengths?	What are our weaknesses?	What are areas of concern?

notes

Citations

RESOURCES ✳ REFERENCES

Resources

MARRIAGE

Capture Her Heart: Becoming the Godly Husband Your Wife Desires, Lysa TerKeurst

Capture His Heart: Becoming the Godly Wife Your Husband Desires, Lysa TerKeurst

Christian Marriage: The New Challenge, David M. Thomas

Fighting for Your Marriage: Positive Steps for Preventing Divorce and Preserving a Lasting Love, Howard J. Markham, Scott M. Stanley, & Susan L. Blumberg

ForYourMarriage.org

Humanae Vitae, Pope Paul VI

Marriage: Love and Life in the Divine Plan, USCCB, U.S. Bishops' Pastoral Letter on Marriage

Take Back Your Marriage: Sticking Together in a World That Pulls Us Apart, William H. Doherty

The Case for Marriage: Why Married People Are Happier, Healthier, and Better Off Financially, Linda Waite & Maggie Gallagher

The First Five Years of Marriage: Launching a Lifelong, Successful Relationship, Wilford Wooten & Phillip Swihart

The Seven Principles for Making Marriage Work, John M. Gottman & Nan Silver

The Treasure of Staying Connected for Military Couples, Janel Lange

Thriving Marriages, John Yzaguirre & Claire Frazier-Yzaguirre

Toward Commitment - A Dialogue About Marriage, Diane & John Rehm

COMMUNICATION AND CONFLICT RESOLUTION

His Needs, Her Needs, Dr. Willard F. Harley, Jr.

Love and Anger in Marriage, David Mace

PMAT: Perfect Marriage Aptitude Test, Mary T. Carty

The Five Love Languages: How to Express Heartfelt Commitment to Your Mate, Dr. Gary Chapman

The Other Side of Love: Handling Anger in a Godly Way, Gary Chapman

You Don't Have to Take It Anymore: Turn Your Resentful, Angry, or Emotionally Abusive Relationship Into a Compassionate, Loving One, Steve Stosny

FAITH & SPIRITUALITY

Blessing Your Husband, Debra Evans

God Knows Marriage Isn't Always Easy, Maureen Rogers Law

Rediscover Catholicism, Matthew Kelly

CHILDREN

Love Sex and Babies: How Your Marriage Can Benefit from Natural Family Planning, Jason Evert

Rekindle the Passion While Raising Your Kids, Anthony Garascia

Remarried with Children: Ten Secrets for Successfully Blending and Extending Your Family, Barbara Lebey

INTIMACY

10 Great Dates to Energize Your Marriage, CLAUDIA & DAVID ARP

A Sense of Sexuality: Christian Love and Intimacy, EVELYN & JAMES D. WHITEHEAD

Good News About Sex and Marriage, CHRISTOPHER WEST

The Way to Love Your Wife: Creating Greater Love and Passion in the Bedroom, CLIFFORD L. PENNER & JOYCE J. PENNER

Theology of the Body: Human Love in the Divine Plan, BL. POPE JOHN PAUL II

COMMITMENT

Breaking the Cycle of Divorce: How Your Marriage Can Succeed Even if Your Parents' Didn't, JOHN TRENT, PH.D.

The Power of Commitment: A Guide to Active Lifelong Love, SCOTT M. STANLEY & GARY SMALLEY

FINANCES

7 Steps to Becoming Financially Free, PHIL LENAHAN, VERITASFINANCIALMINISTRIES. COM

The Total Money Makeover: A Proven Plan For Financial Fitness, DAVE RAMSEY, DAVERAMSEY.COM

CEREMONY

CatholicBrides.com

MARRIAGE ENRICHMENT

MARRIAGE ENCOUNTER, **www.wwme.org**

PREPARE/ENRICH, **www.prepare-enrich.com**

RETROUVAILLE, **www.retrouvaille.org**

References

1 Divorce Law Needs No Tweaking. (2005, March 7). Atlanta Journal Constitution.

2 Sharp Increase in Marriages of Teenagers Found in 90's. (2002, November 9). *New York Times*. Retrieved from the Smart Marriages Archive.

3 DiCaro, V. (2005). NFI Releases Report on National Marriage Survey. *Fatherhood Today*, 10:3. Retrieved from www.fatherhood.org.

4 Markey, B. (2009). Dealing with Risk Factors of Interfaith Marriages. Retrieved from Smart Marriages Online conference notes: divorcereform. org/stats.html.

5 Divorce, American-Style [Electronic version]. (1999). *Scientific American*, 280 (3).

6 Cohabitation Data. (1999). www.smartmarriages.com/ cohabit.html.

7 Cohabitation, Marriage, Divorce, and Remarriage in the United States [PDF document]. (2002). *Vital and Health Statistics, Series Report, 23* (22). Retrieved from www. cdc.gov/nchs/data/series/sr_23/ sr23_022.pdf.

8 Lichter, D.T., et al. (1992). Race and the retreat from marriage: A shortage of marriageable men? [Electronic version]. *American Sociological Review*, 57: 781-799.

9 Glenn, N.D. & Kramer, K.B. (1991). The marriages and divorces of the children of divorce [Electronic version]. *Journal of Marriage and the Family*, 49: (811-825).

10 Popenoe, D. (2002). Debunking Divorce Myths. *The National Marriage Project at Rutgers University*. Retrieved from www.catholiceducation. org/articles/marriage/mf0043. html.

11 A Snapshot of Marriage in the U.S. (2007). U.S. Council of Catholic Bishops: National Pastoral Initiative on Marriage.

12 Rivers, D. (2008) The seven challenges workbook: Cooperative communication skills for success at home and at work, 6th ed. Retrieved from www.newconversations.net/ sevenchallenges.pdf.

13 Banning, B. & Neill, G. (2009). Techniques for effective communication: The checklist. Retrieved from ezinearticles. com/?Techniques-For-Effective-Communication—The-Checklist&id=2403966.

14 Marx-Kelly, D. (2001). Essential skills for marriage: Communication. *Counseling for Modern Life*. Retrieved from www.modernlife.org/ Fall2001issue/Communication. htm.

15 Vogt, S. (2009). Common values. Retrieved from foryourmarriage.org/ everymarriage/what-makes-marriage-work/common-values.

16 Wilcox, W.B. (2005, October). Seeking a soulmate: A social scientific view of

the relationship between commitment and authentic intimacy. Proceedings from *A Colloquium of Social Scientists and Theologians*. Retrieved from old.usccb.org/laity/marriage/Wilcox.pdf.

17 Pope Paul VI. (1965). *Gaudium et Spes: Pastoral Constitution on the Church in the Modern World*. Retrieved from www.vatican.va/archive/hist_councils/ii_vatican_council/documents/vat-ii_const_19651207_gaudium-et-spes_en.html.

18 Pope Paul VI. (1964). *Lumen Gentium: Dogmatic Constitution on the Church*. Retrieved from www.vatican.va/archive/hist_councils/ii_vatican_council/documents/vat-ii_const_19641121_lumen-gentium_en.html.

19 The Catholic Bishops of Pennsylvania. (1999). Living Together. Retrieved from www.ewtn.com/library/BISHOPS/LVNGTGTH.htm.

20 Badger, S. (2005). Ready or not?: Perceptions of marriage readiness among emerging adults. Unpublished doctoral dissertation, Brigham Young University.

21 Magarrell, R.L. & D.E. Barley. (2005). Breaking the chain of negative family influences. *Marriage and Family, Summer*.

22 Amato, P.R. (1996). Explaining the intergenerational transmission of divorce. Journal of Marriage and Family, 58(3), 628-640. Retrieved from www.jstor.org/pss/353723.

23 Bryant, C. M., R.D. Conger, & J.M. Meehan. (2001). The influence of in-laws on change in marital success. Journal of Marriage and Family, 63(3), 614-626. Retrieved from www.jstor.org/pss/3654637.

Throughout the workbook:
Catholic Church. (1997). *Catechism of the Catholic Church*, 2nd ed [Electronic version]. Vatican: Libreria Editrice Vaticana.

Of related interest

LETTERS TO A YOUNG MARRIED COUPLE

Practical Wisdom and Guidance for the Newly Married

KATHY F. HASTY

This beautiful book is a series of short letters written to newlyweds, offering wisdom and practical advice as a way of companioning those starting out on the sacred journey of marriage. Through this book, the author's hope is to walk with the reader as a friend, giving reflections in each letter and then inviting the couple to explore each topic further through the discussion questions provided.

112 PAGES | **$12.95** | 5½" X 8½" | **9781627852548**

WHAT POPE FRANCIS SAYS ABOUT MARRIAGE AND FAMILY LIFE

30 Days of Reflections and Prayer

Every married couple can look to Pope Francis as a caring spiritual director who offers both profound wisdom and sensible advice for daily living. Spend 30 days here with Pope Francis, reflecting on marriage and family. Let his words help you discover how God's grace envelops your family with love, now and forever.

32 PAGES | **$1.95** (BULK PRICING AVAILABLE) | 4" X 6" | **9781627850896**

POCKET PRAYERS FOR MARRIED COUPLES

PATRICIA HUGHES BAUMER, M.DIV. & FRED A. BAUMER, PH.D.

This timeless treasury of prayers will be cherished by married couples and handed down lovingly from one generation to the next. Each section of prayers focuses on a different phrase of the wedding vows—I take you, to have and to hold, from this day forward, in joy and in sorrow (for better or for worse), for richer, for poorer, in sickness and in health, until death do us part—and applies it to real-life situations, helping couples pray throughout their marriage and helping them remember that God is always with them.

80 PAGES | **$9.95** | 4" X 6" | **9781627850711**

PREPARING FOR A LIFETIME OF LOVE

*30 Reflections for Engaged Couples from Pope Francis' **The Joy of Love***

Drawn from the parts of *The Joy of Love* in which Pope Francis speaks directly to couples, the thirty brief reflections here help couples remember what is most important about their wedding and marriage—now and throughout their lives together.

32 PAGES | **$2.95** (BULK PRICING AVAILABLE) | 4" X 6" | **9781627852333**

WHY GET MARRIED IN THE CHURCH

The Lifelong Blessings of a Catholic Wedding

JOHN BOSIO

This warm and welcoming book invites engaged couples to discover the grace, mystery, strength, and wonder of the Catholic sacrament of marriage and provides honest answers to commonly asked questions. More importantly, it explains the deeper purpose of marriage as a vocation, and how couples can draw unique grace and strength from the sacrament, their faith, and the entire Catholic community.

24 PAGES | **$1.95** (BULK PRICING AVAILABLE) | 5½" X 8½" | **9781585959075**